Pulling Taffy

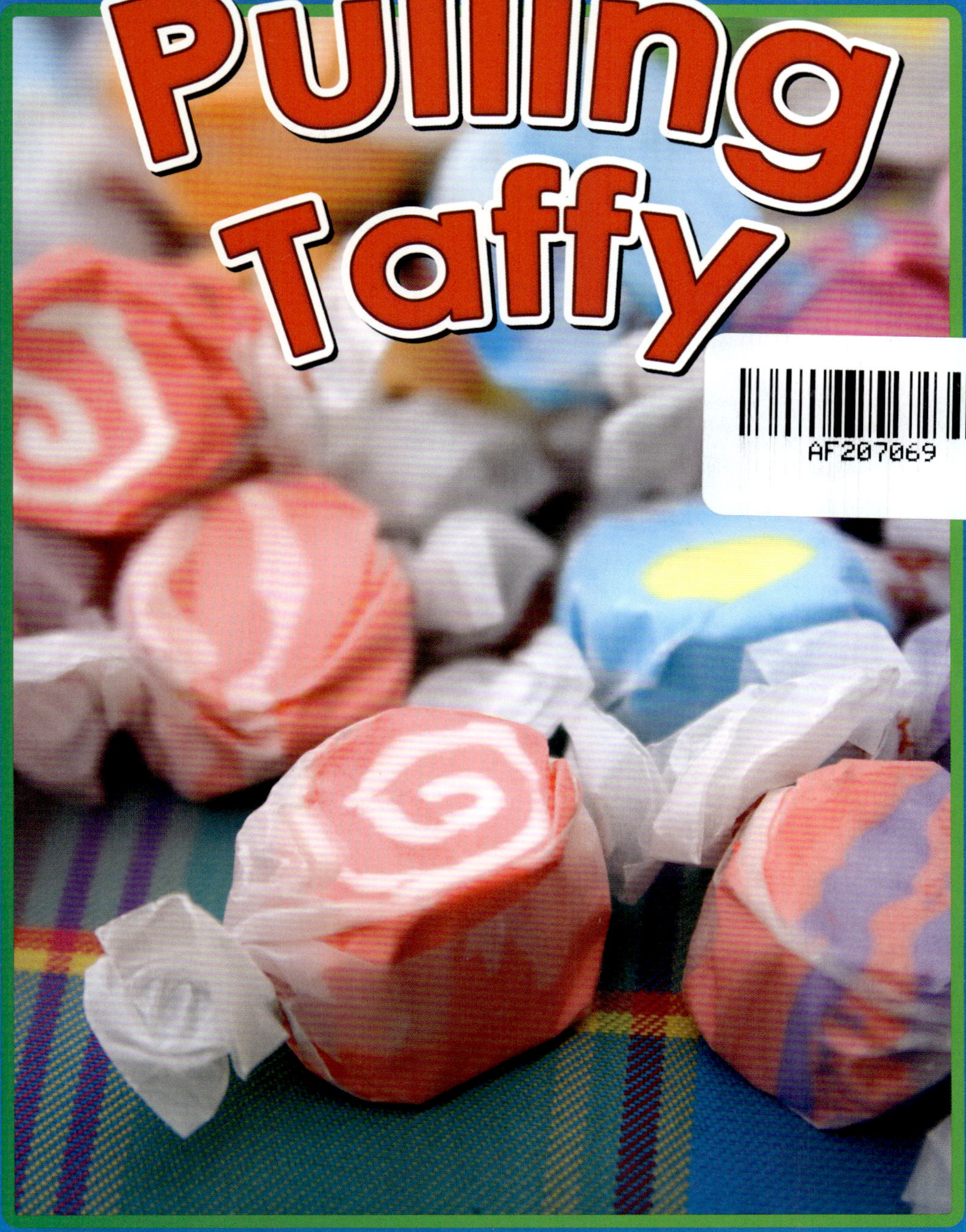

Anne Montgomery

Taffy is a candy. It was first made at the beach.

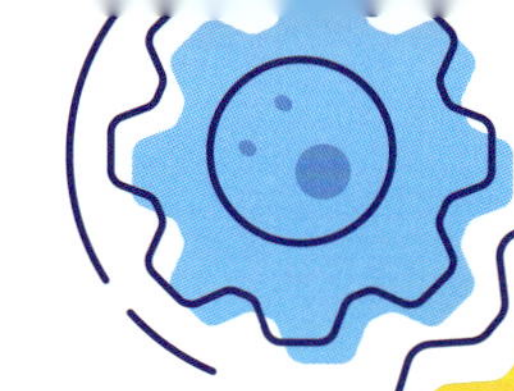

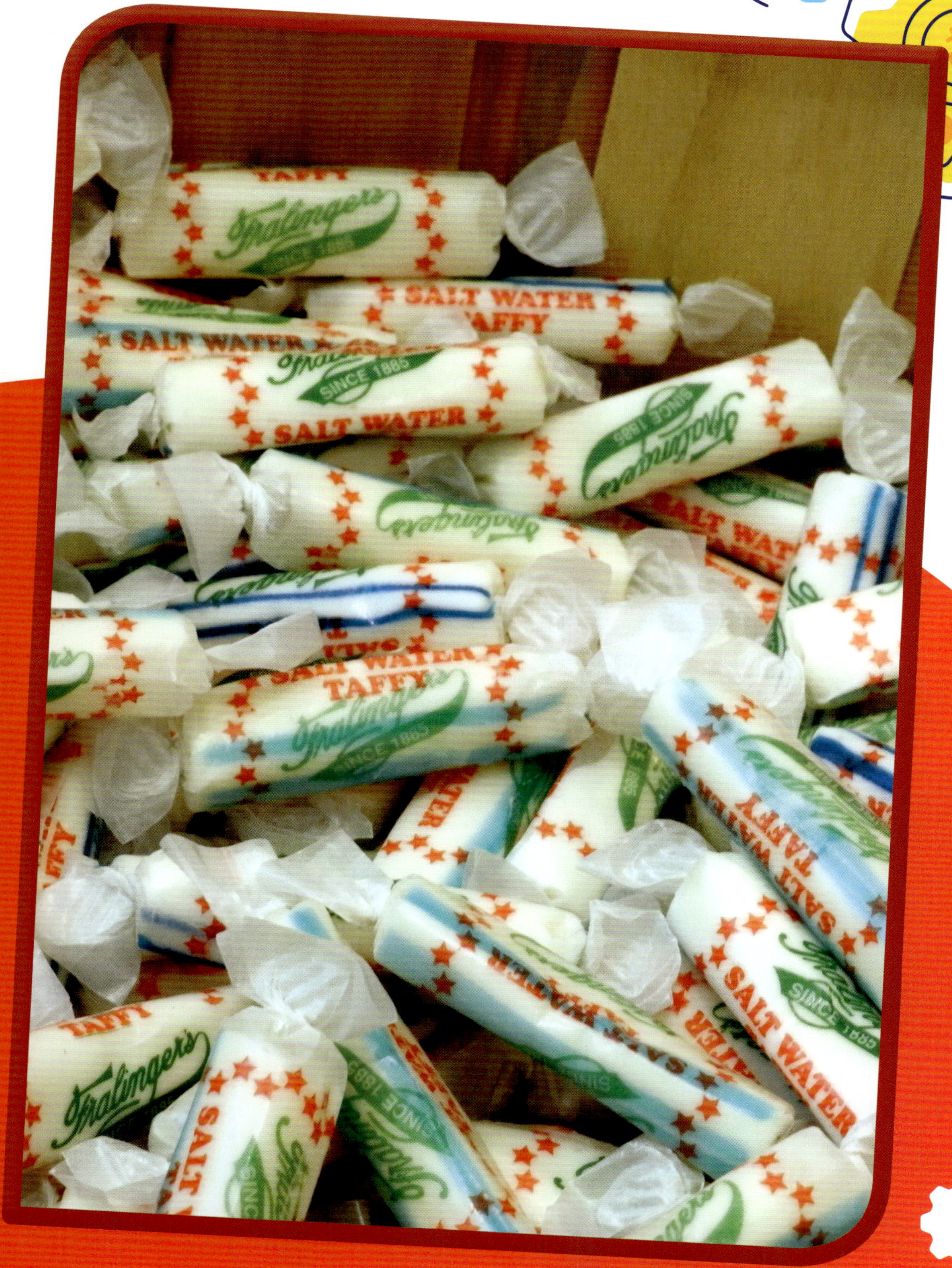
Fralinger's
SINCE 1885
SALT WATER
TAFFY

People loved taffy. They loved to watch it being made.

4

They still love it. But machines help make it now.

Taffy is made with these foods.

SUGAR
0g High Fructose Corn Syrup
aro
CORN SYRUP
WITH REAL VANILLA
FL OZ. (1 PL) 473ml
BUTTER
NET WT. 4 OZ • 113 g
BUTTER
ml
1200
1100
1000
900
800
700
600
500
400
300
200
100
2
1¾
1½
1¼
1
¾
½
¼
pts.
fl. oz.
40
35
30
25
20
15
10
5

This machine folds the taffy. It mixes in air.

10

This machine rolls the taffy. It keeps it soft.

This machine cuts the taffy. It wraps it too.

14

HAND DIPPED ICE CREAM

Then we get to eat the taffy!   Yum!

STEAM CHALLENGE

The Problem

Taffy should stretch without breaking. What is the best way to pull taffy so it doesn't break?

The Goals

- Make some putty.
- Roll, pull, and stretch your putty.
- It should stretch without breaking.

1 Research and Brainstorm
Learn about taffy.

2 Design and Build
Plan how you will roll or pull your putty. Make the putty!

3 Test and Improve
Roll or pull your putty. Then, try to stretch it more.

4 Reflect and Share
What did you learn?

Consultants

Amy Zoque
STEM Coordinator and Instructional Coach
Vineyard STEM School
Ontario Montclair District

Siobhan Simmons
Marblehead Elementary
Capistrano Unified School District

Publishing Credits

Rachelle Cracchiolo, M.S.Ed., *Publisher*
Conni Medina, M.A.Ed., *Editor in Chief*
Diana Kenney, M.A.Ed., NBCT, *Series Developer*
Emily R. Smith, M.A.Ed., *Content Director*
Véronique Bos, *Creative Director*
Robin Erickson, *Art Director*
Stephanie Bernard, *Associate Editor*
Mindy Duits, *Senior Graphic Designer*
Smithsonian Science Education Center

Image Credits: p.3 PL Gould/Shutterstock; p.5 ClassicStock/Alamy; p.7 Carl D. Walsh/Getty Images; p.11 Herb Swanson/Portland Press Herald via Getty Images; p.13 Kris Tripplaar/Sipa USA/Newscom; p.15 Jeramey Lende/Shutterstock; all other images from iStock and/or Shutterstock.

Library of Congress Cataloging-in-Publication Data
Names: Montgomery, Anne (Anne Diana), author. | Smithsonian Institution.
Title: Pulling taffy / Anne Montgomery.
Description: Huntington Beach, CA : Teacher Created Materials, Inc., [2019] |
   "Smithsonian Institution."--Copyright statement. | Audience: Age 5. |
   Audience: K to grade 3. |
Identifiers: LCCN 2018055266 (print) | LCCN 2018059315 (ebook) | ISBN
   9781425859862 (eBook) | ISBN 9781493866410 (pbk.)
Subjects: LCSH: Candy--Juvenile literature.
Classification: LCC TX792 (ebook) | LCC TX792 .M65 2019 (print) | DDC
   641.85/3--dc23
LC record available at https://lccn.loc.gov/2018055266

✳ Smithsonian

Teacher Created Materials

5301 Oceanus Drive
Huntington Beach, CA 92649-1030
www.tcmpub.com
ISBN 978-1-4938-6641-0

20